Contents

Any words appearing in the main text in bold, **like this**, are explained in the Glossary. You can also look out for them in the Star words box at the bottom of each page.

A shining star

In the film world nothing tops winning an Oscar. In 2001 Halle Berry played a waitress in the film *Monster's Ball*. It was a great performance and Halle was **nominated** for the best actress Oscar. That year there were lots of good actresses up for the Oscar. These included Nicole Kidman and Renée Zellweger. Many people thought Halle had no chance of winning.

Oscar history

On 24 March 2002 Halle made history. She became the first African American woman to win the Oscar for best actress. She heard her name being called and her eyes filled with tears. It did not seem real.

★ ★ ★ ★ ★ ★ ★ ★ ★ ★ ★

Halle's Oscar speech, 2002

'Oh, my God. Oh, my God. I'm sorry. This moment is so much bigger than me. This moment is for… every nameless, faceless woman of colour that now has a chance because this door tonight has been opened.'

★ ★ ★ ★ ★ ★ ★ ★ ★

ALL ABOUT HALLE

Full name: Halle Maria Berry
Born: 14 August 1966
Place of birth: Cleveland, Ohio, USA
Family: Father: Jerome Berry; Mother: Judith Berry; Sister: Heidi Berry
Height: 5' 6" (1.68 metres)
Hobbies: Roller-blading, shopping
Married: David Justice (married 1 January 1993, divorced 1996);
Eric Benét (married 24 January 2001, divorced 2004)
Big break: Halle's first film role was in Spike Lee's *Jungle Fever* (1991)
Major films: *X-Men* (2000), *Monster's Ball* (2001), *Die Another Day* (2002), *X-Men 2* (2003), *Gothika* (2003)
Other interests: Collecting art

Star words

nominate put forward as one of the people to win an award

Find out later

Hope for black women

When Halle went on to the stage she whooped and screamed with joy. She knew this was an important moment for her. It was also important for African Americans in film.

The great movie star

That night Halle Berry looked like a great movie star. Since then she has not looked back. In 2002 she starred in the James Bond film *Die Another Day*. The following year she appeared in *X-Men 2* and *Gothika*. Halle not only looks good on the screen, she works hard to make the characters she plays feel real. This is why audiences love to watch her.

Who gave Halle her big break?

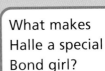

What makes Halle a special Bond girl?

Which comic book character has Halle brought to life?

Halle raises her Oscar into the air at the Academy Awards in 2002.

Halle's heroine

Halle was born at Cleveland City Hospital. Dorothy Dandridge (shown below) had been born there in 1922. Dorothy was a famous African American actress. She starred in the film *Carmen Jones*. In 1955 Dorothy was nominated for an Oscar for her part in the film. Dorothy is an inspiration to Halle. When Halle won the Oscar she remembered her heroine.

★ ★ ★ ★ ★ ★ ★ ★ ★ ★

A star is born

How many people have the same name as a shop? Halle was named after the department store Halle Brothers. Her mother liked the sound of the name. This store was in her home town of Cleveland, Ohio, USA. Halle's name makes her stand out as different. Her early life was different, too, but it was not always happy.

Halle's parents

Halle's mother Judith was born in Liverpool, England. She moved to the USA when she was six. Judith and Jerome Berry met and fell in love at a hospital in Cleveland. Jerome was a hospital worker. Judith was a **psychiatric nurse**. He was African American and she was white. At this time, **inter-racial relationships** were unusual. The couple often faced racist comments. Even so they got married. In 1962 they had a daughter called Heidi. Four years later they had Halle.

Halle's heroine is the 1950s movie star Dorothy Dandridge.

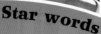
Star words   **psychiatric nurse** nurse who looks after people with mental illness

An unhappy home

By the time Halle was born her father was drinking a lot. Halle remembers seeing her father throw their dog against the wall. When Halle was four, Judith threw Jerome out of the family house. Halle's mother is a strong character. She has always been an **inspiration** to Halle.

Halle's father

'When somebody mentions my father, that's the first thing I think about – that dog flying across the room. I remember saying, "… let him leave!"'

Halle's home town of Cleveland is the business centre for Ohio.

inter-racial relationship relationship between people from different races

Mixed blessings

Halle's mother Judith worked hard to look after her young daughters. She wanted their lives to be as normal as possible. Then, in 1976, their father Jerome moved back home. Very soon he began to drink again. This time Judith threw him out and told him not to come back.

New start

That year Judith and the girls moved to Oakwood Village. This was a **suburb** of Cleveland. The area was nearly all-white. Halle had to face racist comments. Some children at school called her 'pug nose'. They said she must be **adopted** because her mother was white. These comments hurt Halle.

Halle's mother Judith helped her become a strong person.

A hard childhood

Halle says of her childhood: 'I always had a feeling of not being enough and that came from my father leaving'.

Getting tough

Judith gave her daughters tough advice about racism. She said that people would treat them as black even though their mother was white. They had to think of themselves as black. Since then Halle has always thought of herself as an African American.

Star words   suburb outskirts of a city where people live

8

Self belief

Judith's wise words and Halle's belief in herself meant that she did well at school. Halle says she is an 'over achiever'. That means she always wants to do better than her best.

> I wanted the best grades. I wanted to be the best at everything.

Early struggles

When Halle was elected to be **prom queen**, other students said she had fixed the results. Halle was cleared of doing anything wrong but she was still angry.

At high school she was class president and editor of the school magazine. She always found it a struggle, though. Halle wanted to be a cheerleader but people said there had never been a black cheerleader. Halle later became the head cheerleader. There had never been a black **prom queen** either, but in 1984 Halle was voted queen.

A typical cheer-leader used to be white. Halle did her bit to change this.

adopt take legal responsibility to care for a child who is not your own

Brains and beauty

★ ★ ★ ★ ★ ★ ★ ★ ★ ★ ★

Halle's style

Even as a teenager Halle had her own style. In the 1987 Miss World Contest she won the prize for 'best-dressed contestant'.

★ ★ ★ ★ ★ ★ ★ ★ ★ ★ ★

The African American singer and actress Vanessa Williams was Miss America in 1983.

Halle's tears on Oscar night 2002 show that she can be very emotional. She felt very hurt when students said she had fixed the results to become **prom queen**. This made her determined to prove her worth in the future.

Beauty queen

Halle did not know how she was going to be 'a somebody'. She was popular with boys but she never thought she was beautiful. Her boyfriend knew that Halle was special and stood out from other girls. Without telling Halle, he entered her into a **beauty pageant**. When Halle was seventeen she won the 1984 Miss Teen Ohio Beauty Pageant. In 1985 she won the Miss Teen All-American Pageant. She was also runner up in the Miss USA Pageant. In 1986, she entered the Miss World Contest in Hong Kong. She did not win but was a runner-up.

> " Beauty can be used to draw people in. But once you're in you've got to be able to do something. "

Halle's next move

Halle did not just want to be a beauty queen. She used the money she won in the pageants to pay her college fees. After high school Halle went to study at Cuyahoga Community College in Cleveland. She decided she wanted to become a **journalist**. Halle soon found out that journalism is a tough business, though.

Star words   beauty pageant **contest where women are judged on their looks and personality**

She did not like asking people personal questions. Halle had to make a hard decision. She decided to leave college. She also decided to leave her home in Cleveland. She moved to Chicago to try to make it as a model.

★ Star fact

Halle was the first African American to take part in the Miss World competition.

★ ★ ★ ★ ★ ★ ★ ★ ★ ★ ★

Wrong job

Halle soon realized she did not want to be a journalist. Once, she had to interview a family whose house had burned down. Halle upset the family even more when she began crying for them.

★ ★ ★ ★ ★ ★ ★ ★ ★ ★ ★

Halle in the 1986 Miss World contest.

The popular actress Cameron Diaz was also a model before she began acting.

Halle the model

In Chicago, Halle found it hard to make a successful career as a model. She was not tall enough for many jobs. She shared a tiny one-bedroom apartment with another model. They had some hard times. Sometimes they did not have enough money to buy food.

Acting classes

Halle won some jobs as a model, but she found the work boring. She dreamed of being an actress so she began acting classes. Vincent Cirrincione was a New York talent agent and film **producer**. He saw Halle in a video of a **beauty pageant**.

Career moves

Other models have moved on to become actresses, including Cameron Diaz, Andie MacDowell and Jessica Lange. Supermodels who have tried acting include Cindy Crawford and Claudia Schiffer.

Halle in the TV series *Living Dolls*.

Star words

diabetes disease that creates high levels of sugar in the blood

He thought that Halle could be a star. In 1989 Halle moved to New York. She lived with Vincent and his wife and went to **auditions** for acting work.

A new look

One day Halle surprised Vincent with a new haircut. Her long curly hair was gone. In its place was the short style for which Halle is famous. The new look helped win her first acting role. In 1989 Halle played a model in a US television series called *Living Dolls*. The series did not take off, but Halle was on her way.

Collapse on set

One day Halle collapsed while filming *Living Dolls*. She was rushed to hospital. She found out that she had **diabetes**. This can be a serious disease. For many years Halle had to inject **insulin** every day to keep well. Now Halle controls her diabetes by eating well and taking regular exercise.

Halle's recipe for keeping well

Exercise

Meditate to avoid stress

Eat lots of vegetables

Eat lots of fruit

Avoid sugar and fried foods

Halle's diet includes lots of healthy fruit and vegetables.

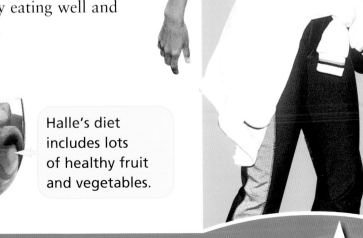

insulin hormone that controls the amount of sugar in the blood. People with diabetes have to be given extra insulin.

The film director Spike Lee.

★ ★ ★ ★ ★ ★ ★ ★ ★ ★ ★

Spike Lee

Spike Lee is famous for his hard-hitting films. Many of his films are about African American people and racial issues. One of his most famous films is about the **civil rights** leader Malcolm X.

★ ★ ★ ★ ★ ★ ★ ★

Halle in her first role in *Jungle Fever*.

The big break

It can be hard for African American actors to find good parts. There are not always many opportunities on television or in films. Halle was out of work for six months when *Living Dolls* ended. Then she got her big break. Spike Lee was a young and talented African American film **director** in Hollywood. He decided that he wanted Halle to work with him on his new film.

Jungle Fever

In 1991, Spike Lee was looking for actors to be in his new film. This was a film about racial issues called *Jungle Fever*.

> " What's the difference between Hollywood characters and my characters? Mine are real. (Spike Lee) "

Star words   director person who is in charge of making a film

The main story in the film was about a love affair between an African American architect and his Italian American secretary. Wesley Snipes played the architect. Another story in the film is about the architect's brother, played by Samuel L. Jackson. He is a drug addict. Halle played another drug addict in the film.

Life on the street

Halle fought hard to get her role in the film. Spike thought she was too beautiful for the part. Halle really wanted the job. It would show people that she was more than a pretty face. To prove her point she did not bathe for ten days before the **audition**. Spike eventually gave her the part. Halle decided to prepare for the role properly. She went to live on the streets. She met real street people. She saw for herself how tough their lives were.

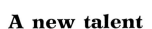

A new talent

Halle learned a lot from her time living on the streets. This made the character she played seem real. She only had a small part in the film but she stood out in all of her scenes. This was not just because of her stunning looks. It was because she could really act, too.

Wesley Snipes is a major Hollywood actor. He has starred in big films like *Blade*.

★ ☆ ★ ☆ ★ ☆ ★ ☆ ★ ☆

Taking risks

Halle wore a bullet-proof jacket when she lived on the streets. It was very dangerous. Halle says she would not take those risks again to get a part.

★ ☆ ★ ☆ ★ ☆ ★ ☆ ★ ☆

15

First roles

Halle in the film *The Last Boy Scout*.

Jungle Fever came out at the beginning of 1991. This was a good year for Halle's career. By the end of 1991 she had starred in three films. *Strictly Business* was her first **big budget** film. She did not have a large part, but she acted well. She was also in *The Last Boy Scout* with action hero Bruce Willis. Again, Halle did not have a big role.

Star fact

For Halle, 1991 had its ups and downs. Her boyfriend punched her in the head. She lost 80 per cent of the hearing in her left ear.

Star words

big budget large amount of money available to spend. A big budget film is made using a lot of money.

Halle's character died early in the film. One thing was clear though, she really shone in front of the camera.

Boomerang

In 1992 Halle starred in the film *Boomerang*. She acted with Hollywood star Eddie Murphy. The film was a romantic comedy. It was fresh and exciting. It was about African Americans working in business. The people in the film were not living tough lives in the 'hood. They were getting rich in advertising. Halle wanted to be in this film because it showed African Americans in a positive way.

Eddie's number one

This time Halle did not have to try too hard to get the part. In the film, Eddie plays a rich **advertising executive**. Halle **auditioned** to play his secretary. Eddie often decides who acts in his films. Halle was the first actress he saw. He was very impressed and refused to see any other actresses.

Halle was pleased to win her part in *Boomerang*.

Eddie Murphy started as a stand-up comedian and became a hugely successful film actor.

advertising executive person with a senior job in an advertising company

Television star

Many actors do not like working for television once they have been in films. Halle has a different attitude. If a story is important then it does not matter where it is told. Halle made a name for herself as a film actress but she was also appearing on television. From 1991 to 1992 she was in the US soap opera *Knots Landing*.

Star of the show

Halle played her first lead role in the 1993 US television drama *Queen*. Halle thought this story was important because it was about African slaves in America. The story was by Alex Haley. He wrote another famous book called *Roots*. In *Queen* Haley wrote about his grandmother. She was **descended** from a white Irish sea captain and an African slave. Halle knew what it was like to be of mixed race. She fought hard to get the part. She acted very well and got some fantastic reviews.

Acting pains

Halle has had several accidents while filming. She injured her back in a horse-riding accident while she was making *Queen*. She also discovered that acting can hurt in other ways, too. In *Queen* her character is slapped and attacked by her white lover. These scenes reminded Halle of being a child and seeing her parents fight. Halle says that the tears she shed on screen were often real.

Alex Haley wrote *Roots* and *Queen*. His novels explore the history of African Americans.

Star words

descendant blood relative. You are descended from the earlier generations of your family.

Halle appeared on the show *Frasier* with Kelsey Grammer.

Guest star

Halle made a small appearance in the television comedy *Frasier*. She was in an episode in 1993 called 'Room Service'. She played Betsy, a caller to Frasier's radio show.

Halle in the television drama *Queen*.

Moving up

I don't believe it!

Halle makes loud snorting sounds when she laughs. She says, 'People make fun of it, then I realize that I do snort like a pig and I get really embarrassed.'

Halle is well-known for her mad laugh.

While she was filming *Queen* Halle fell in love with the baseball player David Justice. He was the star player for the Atlanta Braves. Halle saw him while she was watching MTV. She liked what she saw. A few weeks later, by chance, David asked a **journalist** friend to get Halle's **autograph**. As well as her autograph Halle sent David her telephone number. An hour passed and David was on the phone.

Being a wife

Halle and David were married just seven months later, on New Year's Day 1993. At twenty-six years old Halle was juggling being a wife and a rising star. David's work was in Atlanta, in the south of the USA. That is where they set up home. Halle's work often took her to Los Angeles, on the west coast of the USA. Eventually they bought a house together in L.A. but their work meant that they were often in different parts of the country.

> Halle says about David Justice: I knew the minute I saw him face-to-face that I was going to marry him.

A good role model

In 1993 Halle starred in the films *CB4*, *Father Hood* and *The Program*. Halle usually tries to choose parts to prove that she is a serious actress. In terms of their success, none of these films were good choices. They did not get good reviews.

Star words autograph famous person's signature

Halle with her first husband, baseball player David Justice.

Role model

Halle has talked about her part in *The Program* and how she felt being classed as a role model: 'That's sort of my way of giving back ... I'm so lucky that I'm able to work in this industry, so I don't take it lightly. Black youth today desperately need positive images and role models. So I won't do certain movies'.

Nor did they do well at the **box office**. *The Program* was not a success, but Halle was proud of her part. She played the tutor of a college football player. Such good roles did not often come to African American actresses.

David Justice steps up to take a swing at the ball.

box office place where tickets are sold. If a film does well at the box office it means that a lot of people paid to go and see it.

A new role

Halle explains the importance of playing Sharon Stone: 'The fact that these executives at the studio, who are all white males, took the risk to have a black woman as this character says a lot as to where we're going. No, we don't want to be just sex objects or be just beautiful … We're starting to be seen a little bit differently'.

John Goodman played Fred in *The Flintstones*.

Halle as Sharon Stone in *The Flintstones*.

Being Sharon Stone

In 1994 Halle was in the film *The Flintstones*. She played Fred Flintstone's secretary Sharon Stone. The cartoon of *The Flintstones* has been making children laugh since 1960. In the film version the characters are brought to life. The main characters include the loud-mouthed Fred Flintstone and his funny friend Barney Rubble.

Integrating The Flintstones

Halle knew that *The Flintstones* was going to be made into a film. She heard that the **director** could not find the right person to play Sharon Stone. She decided to try for the part. Halle likes serious roles, but she wanted to try comedy.

Star words

integrate bring people together, rather than separate them into different groups

She also wanted to get a part that was not specifically for a black person. She told the director that the Flintstone town of Bedrock needed to be **integrated**.

Researching the role

The Flintstones starred many fine comic actors, including John Goodman and Rick Moranis. Halle was nervous of playing her first comic role alongside such funny men. She researched her part by watching old movies. She learned a lot from the film actress Mae West. Mae had made audiences laugh between the 1920s and 1940s.

A big hit

Halle was a big hit in the role. Sharon Stone was beautiful but **scheming**. The film was a big success, too. It made more than US$100 million at the **box office**. This was the first film that Halle had been in to make so much money.

Halle's favourite food

Treat: Ice cream

Favourite junk food:
Salt and vinegar crisps

Top meal: Grilled tuna with garlic mashed potatoes

Watching Mae West films helped Halle in her role as Sharon Stone.

Halle's **diabetes** means she has to watch her diet carefully, but she cannot resist ice cream.

Winning and losing

In her next films, Halle was back playing serious roles. In *Losing Isaiah* she played a drug addict. Then, in *Executive Decision*, she was a brave flight attendant. On television, she played the Queen of Sheba in *Solomon and Sheba*.

Losing Isaiah

In the film *Losing Isaiah* Halle plays a mother who loses her baby son Isaiah when she becomes addicted to drugs. Her baby is found and **adopted** by a middle-class family. The mother manages to fight her drug addiction. She fights for **custody** of her son and eventually wins him back.

Winning the part

Once again, Halle had a tough **audition**. She nearly did not get the part. The **director** did not think Halle could play such a demanding role. Both the film and Halle got mixed reviews.

★ ★ ★ ★ ★ ★ ★ ★ ★ ★ ★

Jessica Lange

In *Losing Isaiah* Halle starred with Jessica Lange (shown above). Jessica is one of Halle's favourite actresses. Jessica is another ex-model. She has had to work hard to prove herself as a serious actress.

★ ★ ★ ★ ★ ★ ★ ★

Halle plays a recovering drug addict in *Losing Isaiah*.

Star words   custody legal right to look after a child

Halle plays a brave flight attendant in *Executive Decision*.

Halle was still pleased to be in a film that tackled serious race issues. The film looks at white parents adopting black children.

Making a million

Executive Decision is a fast-paced action film. It takes place on a **hijacked** passenger plane. Halle plays a flight attendant. She helps to foil a plot by terrorists. They want to blow up the plane and spread nerve gas over Washington D.C. in the USA. Halle starred with actors Steven Seagal and Kurt Russell. She also became the first African American actress to earn US$1 million for a film. In the same year *People* magazine put Halle in its list of '50 Most Beautiful People'. Halle was flying high.

Opening doors

In 1995, Halle said: 'If I keep getting roles in movies like *The Flintstones* and *Losing Isaiah* in the same year, five years from now I'll be fulfilled as an actress. I'll feel like I've helped open a few doors. And I'll feel like I helped bring some other black women in behind me.'

New face

In 1996 Halle became the new face of a major cosmetics company. She followed in the footsteps of the supermodel Cindy Crawford.

Halle is a serious actress but beauty and glamour are important for her image, too.

Highs and lows

The year 1996 had its highs and lows. Halle always wanted to be a leading lady. She fulfilled this **ambition** in two films that year. Halle was a success on screen but at the same time her marriage was failing.

Race the Sun

In *Race the Sun* Halle plays a teacher at a high school in Hawaii. She **inspires** a group of poor students. They build a prize-winning **solar-powered** car. The film is based on a true story but it was criticized for being corny. *Race the Sun* was a flop at the **box office**, but for Halle it showed that she could be top of the bill.

Rich Man's Wife

Halle's next film was *Rich Man's Wife*. This was a murder mystery. Halle plays the rich, bored wife of the title. Halle liked the role. She played an attractive, but dangerous, woman. She also enjoyed working with a female **director**. The film did not do very well, but by that time Halle had other problems.

It's over

Halle's marriage to David Justice ended in 1996. The couple had struggled with living apart.

After their split Halle became **depressed**. To add to her troubles she was mugged. Her pet dogs were killed by coyotes in her back garden. Her father, who had left home when Halle was a child, tried to contact her. This made her angry.

Halle in *Rich Man's Wife*.

Halle plays a teacher in the inspirational drama *Race the Sun*. Her pupils win a competition to race their car in Australia.

Taking the lead

Halle talks about playing the lead role in films: 'I'd be lying if I said that I didn't feel pressure, but I also know why I'm doing what I'm doing, and I'm really doing this because I love to act.'

★ Star fact

Halle regrets getting a tattoo of David Justice's name. When they divorced in 1996 she had the tattoo changed to a sunflower.

Halle's style

Halle is famous for her glamour and style. She works hard at her image but is happy to share her secrets. Halle has an official website called hallewood.com. On it she recommends beauty products and talks about her favourite clothes. You can even watch video footage of Halle working out with her **personal trainer**.

The workaholic

Halle is a born fighter. She overcame her **depression** about her divorce by working hard.

Back to comedy

Halle tried to put the horrible events of 1996 behind her. She starred in the comedy *B.A.P.S* (Black American Princesses). She plays a waitress who dreams of opening a restaurant and beauty business with her friend. The story follows the girls as they pursue their goal. One of the jokes in the film is that the girls have appalling taste in clothes. Not many people thought the joke was funny. The film was another flop.

Bulworth

Halle starred in the 1998 film *Bulworth*. At last Halle felt that she was on the brink of something big. Hollywood superstar Warren Beatty plays a politician in the movie. Halle plays a woman who has been hired to **assassinate** him. He falls in love with her.

Halle shows off her unique style at the MTV Movie Awards in 2000.

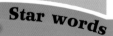
Star words personal trainer person who teaches somebody how to train or exercise on a one-to-one basis

Halle became friends with Warren Beatty when they worked together on *Bulworth*.

Favourite actresses

Halle admires actresses who play strong and serious characters. She also admires comedy actresses.

This was a strong role for Halle. *Bulworth* was a powerful film about race and politics. The film got both good and bad reviews. Many African Americans thought the film showed black people in a negative way. Even so, that year Halle was **nominated** for an award from the **NAACP** for her positive portrayal of an African American in a film.

"She has a great sense of humour about herself. (Warren Beatty on Halle)"

Whoopi Goldberg is one of Halle's favourite actresses.

New beginnings

In 1998 Halle appeared on television and cinema screens. Though none of her work was hit material Halle was falling in love again.

Why Do Fools Fall in Love?

Halle's next role was in the story of Frankie Lymon. He was a singer in the 1950s. He recorded the hit song 'Why do fools fall in love?'. Halle plays Frankie's wife, Zola Taylor. She was lead singer with the group The Platters. Halle was praised for her beauty but the film did not get good reviews.

Halle is a big fan of the sassy singer Tina Turner.

The Wedding

Halle's next part was in the television drama *The Wedding*. She plays the daughter of a rich African American family. Her character is about to get married. She struggles to choose between marrying a poor white jazz musician or a successful African American businessman. Halle picked the role because it broke down **racial stereotypes**.

Halle in the film *Why Do Fools Fall in Love?*

Favourite music

Halle's favourite musicians and performers include: Eric Benét, Norah Jones, D'Angelo, Angie Stone, Tina Turner, Carl Thomas, Mary Mary, DMX, Michelle Williams and Enya.

Star words

racial stereotype when people of a certain race are shown in a fixed and usually negative way

Halle in *The Wedding*.

Halle's adopted daughter

Eric Benét has a young daughter, called India, from an earlier relationship. India's mother had died in a car crash. When Halle and Eric's relationship became more serious, Halle legally **adopted** India.

Halle enjoys a quiet moment with her adopted daughter India.

New love

Around this time, Halle was introduced to the R 'n' B singer Eric Benét. They liked each other but took their relationship slowly. Halle was still getting over her divorce from David Justice. Gradually, the relationship became serious. Halle and Eric moved in together and then became engaged in 1999.

Face of an Angel

Halle always dreamed of filming the story of her heroine, the actress Dorothy Dandridge. First of all, Halle had to win the role. It was a tough competition. Other talented African American actresses wanted the part, including Vanessa Williams and Janet Jackson. In 1999 Halle finally landed the role of Dorothy. She was passionate about the film. She also signed on as executive **producer**.

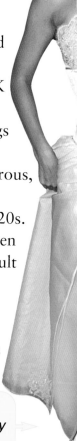

A tragic life

Halle's film was called *Introducing Dorothy Dandridge*. (In the UK it was called *Face of an Angel*.) Halle brings Dorothy back to life. Dorothy was a glamorous, but tragic, figure. Her story begins in the 1920s. She came from a broken home and had a difficult childhood. Dorothy becomes a backing singer and dancer and struggles to succeed as an actress.

Dorothy Dandridge in the 1954 film *Carmen Jones*.

★ ★ ★ ★ ★ ★ ★ ★ ★

An inspiration

Halle had always admired Dorothy Dandridge. Dorothy **inspired** her. Halle said: 'I knew I wanted to be an actress just because of her [Dorothy Dandridge] and how she jumped off the screen'.

★ ★ ★ ★ ★ ★ ★ ★ ★

Halle at the premiere of *Introducing Dorothy Dandridge*.

Star words

segregate separate people according to their race. In the USA in the 1950s, black and white people often lived apart in different areas.

The first black star

The film shows how difficult it was to be a black star in the 1950s. At that time the USA still had **segregation**. In one scene Dorothy is told she must not bathe in the white-only swimming pool at a hotel. Dorothy defies the rule. The pool is emptied and black employees have to scrub the pool 'clean'. Dorothy was nominated for an Oscar for *Carmen Jones*. This was the high point of her career.

Rave reviews

Halle had singing and dancing lessons to play the part of Dorothy. She put lots of emotion into her acting. This comes from her own experience of life and her strong connection with the tragic star. Halle's determination and hard work paid off. In 2000 she won an Emmy award for her part in the film.

Strangely fitting

Halle tried on one of Dorothy's dresses. She found it fitted her perfectly. Halle has a very small waist. This means her dresses often need to be taken in. Dorothy's dress did not need to be altered at all!

Halle with the Emmy she won for playing Dorothy Dandridge.

Reaching the top

Being in X-Men

Halle explains why she chose the part in *X-Men*: 'I love the theme of the film, which is accepting people for who and what they are. That felt really important to me, especially being a minority in this country. Anyone who has ever felt like an outcast will appreciate the story.'

In 2000 Halle appeared in the science-fiction film *X-Men*. She played the character Storm. *X-Men* is based on a Marvel comic story, but it has a serious message about people living together in peace. It was Halle's first film set in a world of fantasy. It was also the biggest **commercial success** so far in her career.

The world of the X-Men

X-Men is set on Earth in what appears to be the future. The story is about a group of people known as 'mutants'. They each have different abilities, depending on their mutation. This sets them apart from ordinary humans. Halle plays a good mutant. Storm has the power to change the weather. There are also villain mutants.

Storms can change the weather and create deadly forks of lightning.

Star words

commercial success something that sells well and makes a good profit

These include Sabertooth, who has super strength and power to crush his enemies. Then there is Toad, who has a superhuman ability to jump.

On top of the Statue of Liberty

Halle looks amazing in the film. Storm's hair looks like bolts of lightning and her eyes glow. In one scene she fights with the mutant Toad on top of the Statue of Liberty.

Playing with the greats

In *X-Men* Halle played alongside great actors like Patrick Stewart and Sir Ian McKellen. The film was praised for its terrific special effects and fantastic costumes. It was a **box office** winner. Now that Halle had played in a real blockbuster she was ready for anything.

Hit and run

In February 2000 Halle was involved in a hit and run accident. Halle drove away from the scene of a serious car accident in which the victim nearly died. Halle claims she temporarily lost her memory and did not remember the crash. She was fined and given 200 hours of **community service**. For a time Halle thought the accident meant the end of her career.

Halle looks electrifying as Storm in the film *X-Men*.

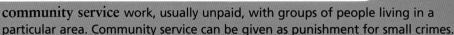

community service work, usually unpaid, with groups of people living in a particular area. Community service can be given as punishment for small crimes.

Popcorn versus art

When you are a star you sometimes get bad press. *X-Men* was a success, but Halle was criticized for taking 'popcorn-movie' roles. A popcorn film is a light, entertaining film that attracts a big audience. In 2001, Halle proved that she could work in both **commercial** films and more serious ones.

> The acting comes first and the looks come second. (John Travolta on Halle)

Swordfish

The film *Swordfish* had top stars and a big budget. John Travolta plays a criminal mastermind. He plots to steal billions of dollars of government money.

A quiet wedding

2001 was special for Halle. It started in the best possible way. She got married to Eric Benét (above) in January. They had a quiet wedding ceremony on a beach in California.

Halle with John Travolta, her co-star in *Swordfish*. John praised Halle and her performance.

Star words   computer hacking illegally entering computer systems

Halle plays his beautiful partner. The movie has bombs, bank robberies, fast car chases and **computer hacking**. Film critics did not like it, and it did not do well at the **box office**.

Monster's Ball

Halle's next film was a different story. It was **low budget** and it has no special effects. Halle plays a waitress who is married to a murderer on **Death Row**. After her husband is executed she struggles to keep her home. Soon afterwards her son is killed in a car crash. She eventually finds love with a prison guard. She does not realize that he was present at her husband's execution.

Painful to watch

Halle worked hard to convince the **director** that she was right for the part. It was the same old story. He thought that Halle was too beautiful for the role. *Monster's Ball* was the performance of Halle's lifetime. Halle claims that she used the pain in her own life to make her character seem more real. Many people find it painful to watch some of the scenes because they are so sad.

Halle plays the waitress Leticia in *Monster's Ball*.

★ ★ ★ ★ ★ ★ ★ ★ ★ ★

An old friend

Rap superstar P. Diddy played Halle's husband in *Monster's Ball*. He and Halle have known each other for more than twelve years. They met when he was part of the crew on the film *Strictly Business*.

★ ★ ★ ★ ★ ★ ★ ★ ★ ★

P. Diddy showed his serious side in *Monster's Ball*.

Death Row section in a US prison where the prisoners have been sentenced to death

Oscar glory

Halle received the best reviews of her career for *Monster's Ball*. She was still surprised to be **nominated** for an Oscar. She never dreamt that she would go on and win the Oscar, too.

Best actresses

Five other African American women have been nominated for the best actress Oscar:
- Dorothy Dandridge in *Carmen Jones*
- Diana Ross in *Lady Sings the Blues*
- Cicely Tyson in *Sounder*
- Whoopi Goldberg in *The Color Purple*
- Angela Bassett in *What's Love Got To Do With It?*

A teary victory

When Halle made her **acceptance speech** she could hardly speak. When the words came though they just kept coming. Halle seemed to thank everybody, including her mother and husband, for helping her. Some people felt she went on too long but the truth was Halle had not prepared a speech.

★ Star fact

Rock star Elton John gives glamorous parties during the Oscars. Halle was celebrating her win at his party when she received a phone call. Nelson Mandela, ex-president of South Africa, called to congratulate her.

Honouring African Americans

Oscar night 2002 was a big night for African American talent. The Hollywood legend Sidney Poitier was given an award for lifetime achievement. Denzel Washington and Will Smith were nominated for the Oscar for best actor. Denzel went on to win the award. After the show, the winners were photographed together. It was a special moment in film history.

Angela Bassett was nominated for an Oscar for playing Tina Turner in *What's Love Got To Do With It?*.

Star words

acceptance speech speech a person gives when they collect an award they have won

Sidney Poitier with his Oscar in 1963.

Winners

Two African American women have won the Oscar for best supporting actress: Hattie McDaniel in *Gone With the Wind* and Whoopi Goldberg in *Ghost*. African American actor Sydney Poitier won an Oscar for best actor in *Lilies of the Field*.

Halle celebrates her Oscar win with the actor Denzel Washington. Denzel won his award for his part in *Training Day*.

Bond and beyond

★ ★ ★ ★ ★ ★ ★ ★ ★ ★ ★

Bond girls

Other famous Bond girls include:
• Ursula Andress as Honey Ryder in *Dr No* (1962)
• Honor Blackman as Pussy Galore in *Goldfinger* (1964)
• Grace Jones as May Day in *A View to a Kill* (1985)
• Famke Janssen as Xenia Onatopp in *Goldeneye* (1995)
• Teri Hatcher as Paris Carver in *Tomorrow Never Dies* (1997).

★ ★ ★ ★ ★ ★ ★ ★ ★ ★ ★

James Bond films are full of well-known lines. They have the best baddies and the most glamorous women. They are action films with great special effects and amazing stunts. They make millions at the **box office**. Anyone who acts in a Bond film knows that they have hit the big time.

Die Another Day

In 2002 Halle appeared in the Bond movie *Die Another Day*. She played Jinx, an undercover agent. She joined a line-up of successful actresses who have starred in the Bond films.

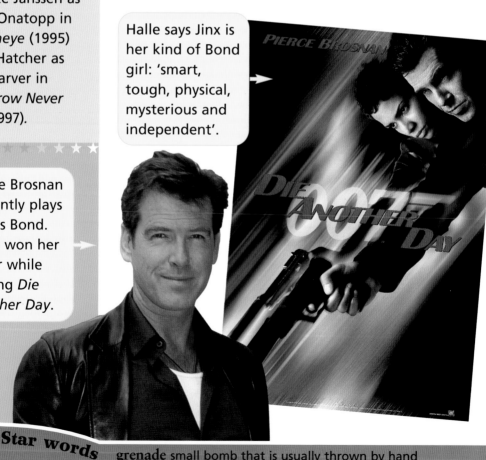

Halle says Jinx is her kind of Bond girl: 'smart, tough, physical, mysterious and independent'.

Pierce Brosnan currently plays James Bond. Halle won her Oscar while filming *Die Another Day*.

Star words   grenade small bomb that is usually thrown by hand

Halle shares a joke with Roger Moore at the London premiere of *Die Another Day*. Roger played Bond in the 1970s and 1980s.

Training for the part

In *Die Another Day* we get to see another side of Halle. It took hours in the gym for her to get fit and strong enough to play Jinx. Being a Bond girl can be dangerous, too. There were rumours that Halle had lost the sight in one eye due to an exploding **grenade**. Fortunately the rumours were not true, but Halle did nearly choke on a fig while filming another scene!

> **She can play an action hero with the best of them.**
> (Pierce Brosnan on Halle)

Halle stands out as Jinx. She is an all-action heroine who is also intelligent and independent. This was a character Halle really enjoyed playing.

International fame

Playing Jinx helped Halle's career. It made her a famous face all around the world. Filming took her to Hong Kong, Cuba, Spain, Hawaii, Iceland and England. The US$4 million she earned was also her biggest pay packet to date.

Magazine polls often vote Halle as one of the most beautiful people in the world.

★ ★ ★ ★ ★ ★ ★ ★ ★ ★

Great beauty

In 2003 *People* magazine voted Halle one of the 50 most beautiful people in the world. Halle has now appeared in the list seven times.

★ ★ ★ ★ ★ ★ ★ ★ ★ ★

Starring roles

Halle continues to shine before the cameras. In 2003 she returned as Storm in *X-Men 2*, the sequel to *X-Men*. Then she appeared in a chilling ghost story called *Gothika*. This time Halle was top of the bill with Hollywood stars Robert Downey Jr and Penelope Cruz.

Halle took the lead role in *Gothika*.

Important stories

Halle has not forgotten about television either. In 2003 she filmed *Their Eyes Were Watching God*. This is based on a famous novel by Zora Neale Hurston. This project is important to Halle because it returns to the subject of race and the struggle to be an African American.

Catwoman

In 2004 Halle took on another comic book role. She starred in the blockbuster film *Catwoman*. The comic book character is independent and carefree. She has the super senses of a cat. It was a role that Halle could really get her claws into! And in 2005 she was the voice of Cappy in the animated movie *Robots*.

Halle plays Storm again in *X-Men 2*.

Another divorce

Halle was going through some sad times again, however. Her marriage to Eric Benét ran into trouble. The couple separated in 2003 and divorced the next year.

An open door

Halle dreamed of being an international star because she wanted to show that African American women can reach the top. To make her dreams come true Halle has had to **strive** with all her heart. Now **producers** and **directors** are queuing up to work with her. She has also 'opened the door' for many other African American actresses.

Halle's salary

Executive Decision (1996) US$1 million
Swordfish (2001) US$2.5 million
Monster's Ball (2001) US$600,000
Die Another Day (2002) US$4 million.
In 2003 Halle was paid about US$8 million per film.

strive work very hard

Find out more

Books

Black Americans of Achievement: Halle Berry, Rose Blue, Corinne J. Naden (Chelsea House Publications, 2001)
Livewire Real Lives: Halle Berry, Julia Holt (Hodder Arnold, 2003)

Filmography

October Squall (due 2006)
Foxy Brown (due 2005)
Nappily Ever After (due 2005)
Robots (2005)
Catwoman (2004)
Gothika (2003)
X-Men 2 (2003)
Die Another Day (2002)
Monster's Ball (2001)
Swordfish (2001)
X-Men (2000)
Why Do Fools Fall in Love? (1998)
Bulworth (1998)
B.A.P.S (1997)
The Rich Man's Wife (1996)
Girl 6 (1996)
Race the Sun (1996)
Executive Decision (1996)
Losing Isaiah (1995)
The Flintstones (1994)
The Program (1993)
Father Hood (1993)
CB4 (1993)

Boomerang (1992)
The Last Boy Scout (1991)
Strictly Business (1991)
Jungle Fever (1991)

Television
Their Eyes Were Watching God (2003)
*Introducing Dorothy Dandridge/Face of an
    Angel* (1999)
The Wedding (1998)
Solomon and Sheba (1995)
Queen (1993)
Knots Landing (1991–92)
Living Dolls (1989)

Websites
http://www.hallewood.com
This is the offical site for Halle Berry. You
will find lots of personal information and
photographs. There is even the opportunity
to email Halle. She tries to answer a few fans'
emails each month.
If you want to find out more about Halle or
her films, a good search engine to try is:
http://www.yahooligans.com

Disclaimer
All the Internet addresses (URLs) given in this book were valid at the
time of going to press. However, due to the dynamic nature of the
Internet, some addresses may have changed, or sites may have ceased
to exist since publication. While the author, packager and publishers
regret any inconvenience this may cause readers, no responsibility
for any such changes can be accepted by either the author, packager
or the publishers.

Glossary

acceptance speech speech a person gives when they collect an award they have won

adopt take legal responsibility to care for a child who is not your own

advertising executive person with a senior job in an advertising company

ambition having something you want to achieve

assassinate plan and carry out the murder of a person

audition interview for a musician or actor, where they show their skills

autograph famous person's signature

beauty pageant contest where women are judged on their looks and personality

big budget large amount of money available to spend. A big budget film is made using a lot of money.

box office place where tickets are sold. If a film does well at the box office it means that a lot of people paid to go and see it.

civil rights the right of everyone to be treated as equals

commercial success something that sells well and makes a good profit

community service work, usually unpaid, with groups of people living in a particular area. Community service can be given as punishment for small crimes.

computer hacking illegally entering computer systems

custody legal right to look after a child

Death Row section in a US prison where the prisoners have been sentenced to death

depressed to be very unhappy

descendant blood relative. You are descended from the earlier generations of your family.

diabetes disease that creates high levels of sugar in the blood

director person who is in charge of making a film

grenade small bomb that is usually thrown by hand

hijack take control of a plane or other vehicle and force the pilot or driver to go somewhere

inspire give someone the idea or motivation to do something

insulin hormone that controls the amount of sugar in the blood. People with diabetes have to be given extra insulin.

integrate bring people together, rather than separate them into different groups

inter-racial relationship relationship between people from different races

journalist somebody who writes for newspapers, magazines or television programmes

low budget small amount of money available to spend. A low budget film does not cost much money to make.

NAACP National Association for the Advancement of Colored People. This group promotes the rights of African Americans.

nominate put forward as one of the people to win an award

personal trainer person who teaches somebody how to train or exercise on a one-to-one basis

producer person who helps to get the money and people together to make a film

prom queen female student who is crowned at the party (called a prom) held in US high schools for graduating students

psychiatric nurse nurse who looks after people with mental illness

racial stereotype when people of a certain race are shown in a fixed and usually negative way

scheme form plots and plans to get what you want

segregate separate people according to their race. In the USA in the 1950s, black and white people often lived apart in different areas.

solar power power from the energy of the Sun's rays

strive work very hard

suburb outskirts of a city where people live

Index